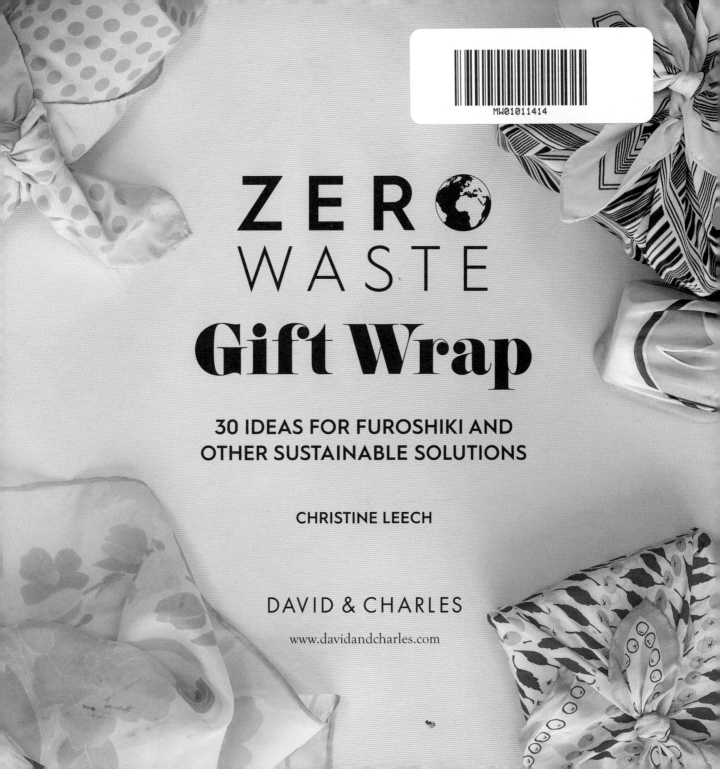

# ZERO WASTE
## Gift Wrap

### 30 IDEAS FOR FUROSHIKI AND OTHER SUSTAINABLE SOLUTIONS

CHRISTINE LEECH

DAVID & CHARLES

www.davidandcharles.com

# Contents

*Dedicated to all the Wombles out there:
making good use of the things that we find...*

# Introduction

*When I was commissioned to write this book I wanted to see just how frugal I could be with materials. I'd made a pact last year to stop buying new clothes and to try and use up my fabric stash before buying more, so this book was the perfect challenge for me. The projects here are the result of one trip to a charity shop and cutting up several pieces from my own wardrobe. I may not have any pyjama bottoms left but I do have all my gift wrapping needs sorted!*

For many years I have gift wrapped presents using the fashion pages from magazines. I liked the way the glossy photos collage into abstract patterns when folded around odd shapes. I also liked that I was doing my bit towards helping the planet by recycling paper and not buying new giftwrap (though there was still sticky tape involved). Then about five Christmases ago I made my sister's family each a set of fabric gift bags. The process of making them was therapeutic. I used old fabrics from my stash and a shrunken jumper and I felt proud I had gone one step further towards a more sustainable lifestyle. These bags come out every year now and I love the challenge of finding gifts to fit inside the very specific sizes!

Fast forward to last Christmas. I was running some Tsutumu and Furoshiki workshops using vintage scarves I had bought from charity shops and kilo sales. Everyone loved the idea of not only giving the present but also an additional gift of a scarf in the wrapping.

So it was perfect timing when I was asked to create this book combining both Furoshiki and other sustainable gift wrapping solutions. The outcome is a mix of large and small projects from simple square wraps and repurposed ribbon rosettes, to gift bags from old shirts, and personalised gift tags.

I hope this book inspires you to go paperless when gift wrapping. I had a lot of fun making the projects and I hope you do too. My personal favourites are the Odd Sock Crackers and the Pyjama Party Bags, plus I now always carry a large silk scarf in my bag to turn into a nifty Katakake Fukuro (or carry wrap) to carry my fruit and veg home.

Happy crafting!

# How to use this book

*I have written this book to inspire and encourage people to think again when faced with a gift-wrapping emergency. Instead of reaching for the shiny, glitter-splashed wrapping paper, look to your wardrobe and fabric stash for wrapping inspiration. This book is divided into the following three sections:*

## THE KNOTS

The eleven projects showcase the Japanese art of Tsutsumu – wrapping gifts using lightweight fabric squares called Furoshiki. There are ideas for wrapping everything from books to bottles, and also for how to create bags - perfect for those awkwardly shaped gifts. The knots work for presents large or small, so you can modify them to suit your needs. I've used wraps from 30cm (12in) up to 75cm (29½in) square.

## THE WRAPS

This section is all about upcycling and using what you already have to create packaging. There are a few projects for making Furoshiki-style wraps and lots of ideas for repurposing items of clothing. Again, the projects are suggestions to inspire you so you will have to adjust the measurements according to your requirements.

## THE EXTRAS

These are present toppers and little bits of pizzazz I've made from fabric scraps left over from the Wrap section. If your fabric is too bulky to tie knots in, gather the corners, fasten them with a hair elastic or safety pin, and add one of these embellishments. Even if you are using paper gift wrap, don't buy plastic ribbon or glittery gift tags – use the ideas in this section to create Fabric Twine, elasticated Scrap Bunting, and things to give your gifts that wow factor.

# Tools and Materials

*The basis of zero-waste crafting is the gathering of recyclable fabric and any other bits and pieces that you can reuse, plus a few simple tools to bring them together.*

## FINDING FABRICS

You may feel squeamish about cutting up perfectly good clothes from charity shops or your own wardrobe. Sadly the rise of fast fashion has meant that charity shops have become overwhelmed with donations, and this clothing often still ends up in landfill as supply outstrips demand. Any clothes repurposed and given a new lease of life in whatever form is always preferable to buying new.

If you are rummaging in the charity shop, think about how much useable fabric you can get from a garment. Pick the largest sizes so you will get the most fabric for your buck. Look out for patch pockets, and shirts with cuffs and plackets, because a stash of those will be invaluable for making small gift bags such as the Pocket Pockets and Shirt Cuff Purses in this book. You'll find you can work with parts of clothing even if it has a few holes, so raid your family's wardrobes and turn that beloved but moth-eaten jumper into a set of heirloom gift bags to be treasured for years to come.

## BASIC SEWING KIT

You will need to have a basic sewing kit, and some yarns and threads in order to turn your re-purposed finds into beautiful gift wrap. I have taken it as read that you have needle and threads, yarn, pins, scissors for thread and fabric, some pinking shears and probably a sewing machine. You will also find it useful to have a stitch unpicking tool, an air-erasable pen and some pretty embellishments like buttons and ribbons. Basic can be beautiful too!

## THINGS TO SAVE

**SCARVES & FABRIC** Silk, rayon, polyester square scarves and large garments made from lightweight fabrics that can be cut into squares.

**RIBBONS & CORD** from paper gift bags and gift boxes.

**T-SHIRTS** Patterned is perfect.

**SHIRTS** Look for nice patterns, with cuffs and patch pockets, decorative buttons are a bonus.

**JUMPERS** Thin knit ones with ribbed cuffs and waistband, cosy Aran ones with chunky patterns, plain ones with an obvious purl stitch.

**DENIM** Jackets with flapped patch pockets, jeans with back pockets and lightweight shirts.

**TROUSERS** Pyjama bottoms and lightweight cotton trousers.

**TIGHTS AND SOCKS** Holed and odd ones are great.

# THE KNOTS

Simple knots and clever folding
make for inspired gift wrap solutions.
Impress your friends and family
with the traditional Japanese art
of Tsutsumu and Furoshiki

# TSUTSUMU & FUROSHIKI

Tsutsumu is the Japanese tradition of wrapping goods and gifts. In Japanese culture giving an unwrapped gift is considered impolite and even the smallest item often comes in a pretty envelope or bag. Larger gifts may be presented wrapped in a Furoshiki.

Furoshiki are traditional Japanese wrapping cloths dating back over 1,200 years, traditionally made from silk or a lightweight fabric. Their use has evolved over this time from wrapping the valuables of emperors to keeping the nobility's clothes off the wet floors of bath houses. In the Edo Period (1603–1868) Furoshiki became the common way for merchants to wrap and carry their goods when out on their deliveries, and for customers to carry their purchases home from the shops. Sadly the rise of the plastic bag in the 1960s saw a decline in the use of Furoshiki, but recently the use of silk scarves as a sustainable yet decorative alternative to wrapping paper has seen a resurgence of the tradition.

## Buying Scarves

When I was a student there was a shop in Bath that sold vintage silk scarves for 50 pence each. I bought loads in different patterns and colours, turning them into pillow cases, summer tops and hair bands. I loved rummaging through the big baskets, the silk cool to the touch as I plunged my hand in deep, hoping to pull out a vintage Hermes or little Chanel number. Now I use my scarf collection to wrap gifts for friends and family. If I've accidentally used one of my favourites, I have been known to ask for it back!

Silk is the traditional fabric for Furoshiki. It folds up small when not in use and its lightness doesn't add bulk to the gifts. Of course other fabrics work well too. Natural fabrics trump man-made ones so look for thin cottons as well as silk when scarf shopping. You'll still get brownie points for shopping vintage so don't feel bad about your polyester and rayon finds. These days I find it hard to get a 50 pence bargain, but the rise of 'kilo sales' have made my shopping trips a lot more fruitful. You can get an Awful Lot of scarves in a kilo (equivalent to 2lb 4oz), definitely enough to keep you knotting all year, plus you get the joy of rummaging through a big bin of fabric treasures.

# REEF KNOT

The reef knot is essential in Furoshiki. It is a neat double knot that is easy to undo.

*I remember learning reef knots when I was in the Brownies, and about six years old. The phrase 'right over left and under, left over right and under' has never left me. Note that I've used different coloured scarves in the photographs to make it clearer. If the ends of your wrap are long, tuck them inside the knot to create a bow shape (see Bunny Wrap project for an example).*

**1** Take the right-hand corner (*blue*) and place it over the left-hand corner (*pink*).

**2** Tie a knot by taking the right-hand corner (*blue*) under the left-hand corner (*pink*).

**3** Notice that the corners have now switched sides. Take the now left-hand corner (*blue*) and place it over the right-hand corner (*pink*).

**4** Tie a second knot by taking the now left-hand corner (*blue*) under the right-hand corner (*pink*).

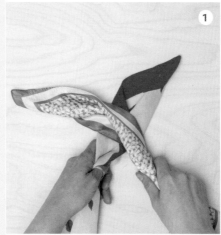

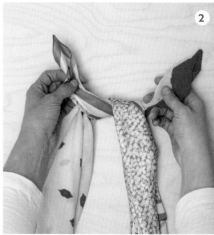

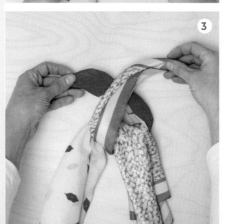

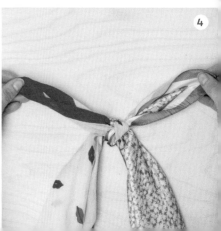

# OTSUKAI TSUTSUMI

**_Translation: basic carry wrap._**
This is the most common type of wrap, and is
good for all sizes of rectangular gift.

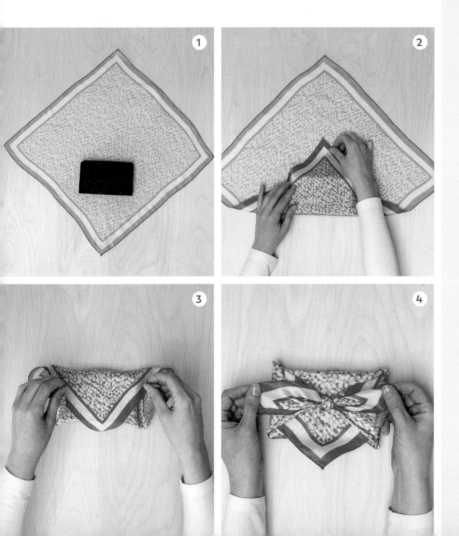

**1** With the scarf set at a
diagonal, Place the gift
below the centre point.

**2** Bring the bottom corner
of the scarf over the gift,
tucking the corner under.
Roll the gift in the scarf
until it is covered.

**3** Lift the left and right
scarf corners.

**4** Tie a reef knot (see Reef
Knot) and manipulate the
scarf ends to look tidy.

# YOTSU MUSUBI

**_Translation: four point wrap._**

This wrap is ideal for boxes. If you have a large enough scarf, twist the ends together after tying the knots to create handles.

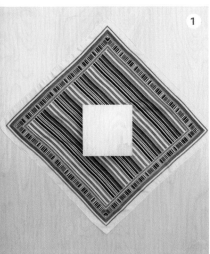

**1** With the scarf set at a diagonal, place the gift in the centre.

**2** Bring the right and left corners together and tie a reef knot (_see Reef Knot_).

**3** Bring the top and bottom corners together and tie another reef knot.

**4** Manipulate the scarf ends to look tidy.

_Note: with a large scarf, tie single knots at steps 2 and 3, twist corners repeatedly, then tie a reef knot to make a handle that stands up._

# FUTATSU TSUTSUMI

**_Translation: two ties._**

Use this wrap for long packages. It's especially useful for gifts in boxes but great for small items of clothing too.

**1** With the scarf set at a diagonal, place the gift lengthways and centrally, then bring the left and right corners together.

**2** Tie a single knot.

**3** Take the corner you are holding in your right hand and hold the bottom corner with your left.

**4** Tie a reef knot (*see Reef Knot*). Repeat with the remaining two corners.

# HON TSUTSUMI

### *Translation: book wrap.*

Perfect when gifting two books, just make sure they are both of a similar size.

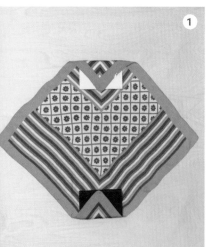

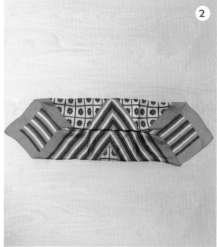

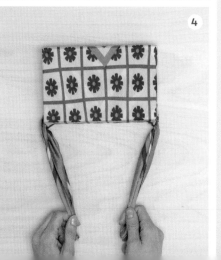

**1** With the scarf set at a diagonal, place the books top and bottom. Fold corners over.

**2** Fold books and scarf into the centre till they meet.

**3** Cross the left and right corners over each other.

**4** Fold the bottom book up onto the top one. Tie the corners in a reef knot (*see Reef Knot*) to make a handle.

# KATAKAKE BUKURO

### *Translation: carry wrap.*

This bag wrap works well for all kinds of gifts,
as long as your gift isn't too heavy.

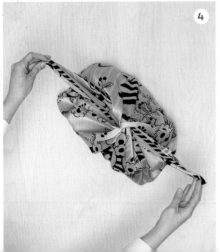

**1** Place the gift in the centre of the scarf.

**2** Tie a single knot in the left and right corners.

**3** Flip both knots so they sit inside the scarf.

**4** Tie the remaining corners with a single knot. Tie a reef knot (*see Reef Knot*) in the ends of the scarf for a handle.

# ODEKAKE BUKURO

***Translation: two handle wrap.***

A large scarf is best for this bag wrap. It's great for gifts and also as a general day bag.

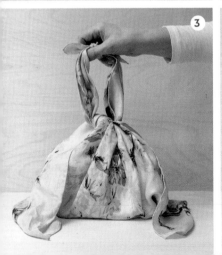

**1** Place the gift in the centre of the scarf.

**2** Take two diagonally opposite corners and tie a single knot.

**3** Tie the corners into a small reef knot (*see Reef Knot*) to create a handle.

**4** Take the other two corners and tie a small reef knot to create a second handle.

# ENTOU TSUTSUMI

***Translation: roll wrap.***

A lovely wrap for cylindrical gifts. Not gifting tins of beans? Then you can always pop a selection of gifts inside a cardboard tube and then wrap that.

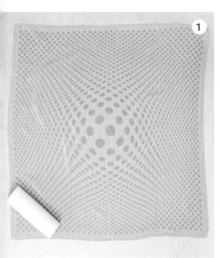

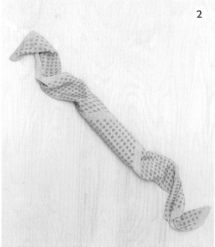

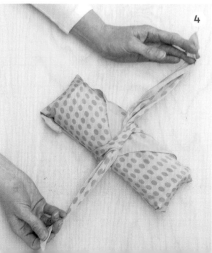

**1** Place the gift at one corner of the scarf.

**2** Roll the gift into the scarf.

**3** Bring together the two long ends of the scarf and tie in a single knot.

**4** Wrap the ends around the gift and tie in a reef knot (*see Reef Knot*) to secure.

# TESAGE BUKURO

**_Translation: hand carry wrap._**
I love the simplicity of this wrap. It is a more open style so if you wish to conceal the gift properly then use a pretty brooch to clip it closed.

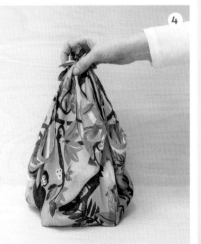

1 Place the gift square in the centre of the scarf.

2 Tie the bottom two corners in a small reef knot (*see Reef Knot*).

3 Repeat with the top two corners.

4 Gather the handles together to carry.

# BIN TSUTSUMI 1

**_Translation: bottle wrap (version 1)._**
Show you really _do_ care by stylishly wrapping that last-minute bottle of wine from the corner shop...

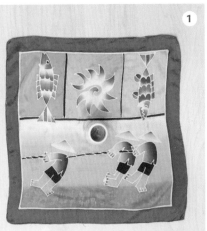

**1** Stand the bottle up in the centre of the scarf.

**2** Tie two diagonally opposite corners together across the top of the bottle with a single knot.

**3** Twist the corners then tie with a small reef knot (_see Reef Knot_) to create a handle.

**4** Cross the remaining two corners and bring to the front of the bottle. Tie with another reef knot.

# BIN TSUTSUMI 2

***Translation: bottle wrap (version 2).***
Ideal for two bottles of the same size. If you're
wrapping wine bottles, use a scarf about
one meter (40in) square.

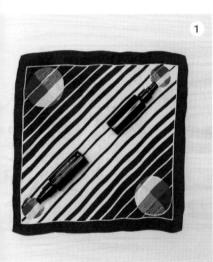

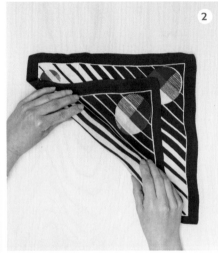

**1** Place the bottles end
to end centrally and
diagonally on the scarf.

**2** Fold the scarf over the
bottles, then roll up the
scarf into a tube shape.

**3** Lift the two corners and
stand the bottles up. You
may need to manipulate
the bottles so they sit
closer together.

**4** Tie with a reef knot (*see
Reef Knot*) to secure.

# OMOTASE BUKURO

### Translation: bracelet bag.

This style of wrapping creates three gifts in one! Not only do you give the gift itself but also the scarf and a pair of bracelets.

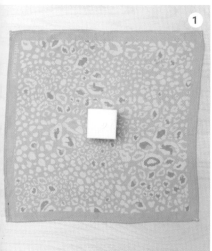

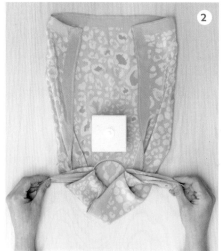

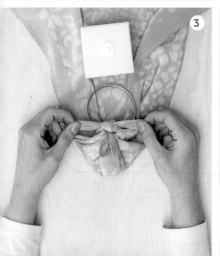

1 Place the gift centrally on the scarf.

2 Thread the two lower corners through one of the bracelets from front to back.

3 Bring the corners round the front of the bracelet and tie a small reef knot (*see Reef Knot*).

4 Repeat with the top two corners and the second bracelet.

# THE WRAPS

Create beautiful everlasting wraps and gift bags by upcycling your old clothing and charity shop finds.

# Sweet Potato Print

This abstract pattern is inspired by the knobbly shape of the potato. No fiddly cutting, just sliced with a knife!

**Prepare the potato.** Cut the potato into different shaped slices. Create stripes by gouging out channels using a lino cutting tool or the corer end of a peeler.

**Prepare the fabric.** Lay a square of fabric onto a flat surface with a bit of give – a stack of newspapers works well. Make sure the fabric is free of creases.

**Prepare the inks.** Start with the paler colours. Squeeze out a decent amount of ink (about 8cm (3¼in) squeezed from a tube) onto your surface and roll it out to a thick layer.

**Print.** Push a fork into the top of your first potato shape for a handle. Press the shape down onto the ink, making sure you get good coverage, practice on a spare piece of fabric first, then place it on the fabric. Press evenly on the potato with your fingers. Remove slowly to avoid smudging. Repeat with each shape and different inks. Finally, add polka dots using the rubber end of a pencil dipped into ink.

**Leave to dry.** Then finish the edges with a machined zig zag stitch or turn and sew a 5mm (¼in) double hem.

## You will need

- Large sweet potato (knobbly is best)
- Sharp knife
- Lino cutting tool or potato peeler
- Pencil with a rubber on the end
- Printing ink or acrylic paints
- Flat surface for rolling ink: old mirror, large tile
- Ink roller
- Fork

"This printed fabric makes great gift tags too. See the method for making them in the Gift Tags project in the Extras section of this book."

# Embellished Wrap

This project is perfect for fabric remnants or outgrown but loved patterned clothing.

## You will need

- Thin patterned material such as Hawaiian shirts or summer dresses
- Air-erasable pen
- Embroidery hoop, threads and needles
- Beaded jewellery, or little packets of sequins from every beaded top you've ever owned!

**Make a square.** Cut your garment into a square shape. Finish the edges by fraying them, or by turning them over 5mm (¼in) twice and then machine sewing to make a double hem.

**Embroider.** Use the pattern on the fabric as a guide for where to add embroidery to your wrap. For precision embroidery placement work out which of the knots you are going to use before embroidering. Wrap the gift and mark the prominent places with an air-erasable pen. Undo the wrap and then embroider. Place the area you wish to work on into the embroidery hoop making sure the fabric is taut and the pattern is not distorted. (*For stitch inspiration see Techniques: Embroidery Stitches.*)

**Embellish.** Add some sparkle to your wrap using your old jewellery and spare sequins. Don't sew any beads at the edges where you will be tying knots.

*"Add a little sparkle to this wrap by adding old earrings or beads from broken necklaces."*

# Crumb Quilt Wrap

Crumb quilting is for people who don't like the precision of traditional quilting, plus it's great for using up all your scraps.

## You will need

- All your fabric scraps
- Scissors or a ruler and rotary cutter
- Matching and contrasting thread

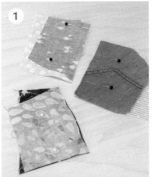

**Prepare the fabric.** Gather all your scraps of fabric together. Ideally each fabric piece will have straight edges, trim away any curved sides. For smaller gifts I tend to use pieces of fabric that are 10cm (4in) or less in size. Pair up different pieces of fabric along one straight edge then pin **(1)**, machine sew with a 5mm (¼in) seam allowance and press all seams open and flat.

**Build the patchwork.** Sort out your paired pieces of fabric and match them up with other pairs, always lining up along one straight edge **(2)**. If any of your joined pieces of fabric don't have straight edges, use a ruler and scissors or a rotary cutter to trim to a straight edge.

**Keep going.** Join and join and join and join your fabric patches together always along a straight edge till you get a square of fabric an appropriate size for your gift. You may need to trim the fabric shape into a square to use as a wrap.

**Hem.** Finish off with either a small 5mm (¼in) double turned hem machine sewn with contrasting thread, or turn once and hem with a zig zag stitch.

*"I've used a ribbon rosette attached to a safety pin to seal this gift, alternatively you could use some fabric twine or an elasticated garland."*

# Natural Dyed Wrap

Warning: this is very addictive. Make sure you have plenty of fabric to experiment with before you start!

## You will need

- Pure cotton, linen or silk fabric squares, edges hemmed or frayed.
- Vinegar
- Turmeric
- Saucepans
- String, pegs, elastic bands
- Plastic gloves

**Prepare the fabric.** Fill a large saucepan with one part vinegar to four parts water. Bring to a medium heat and submerge the fabric. Boil for an hour. This prepares the fabric and helps the dye hold. If you want to guarantee your dye survives machine washes then use a chemical mordant (dye fixer). Otherwise, to be on the safe side, always handwash your wraps with similar colours.

**Make the turmeric dye.** Add two tablespoons of turmeric to 500ml (18fl oz) of water. Bring to the boil and simmer for 20 minutes. Use a saucepan that won't stain!

**Rinse off the fabric.** If you want an all-over colour then keep the fabric flat. Alternatively, concertina and fold the fabric wrapping it tightly with string or secure with pegs for a striped Shibouri pattern **(1)**, or gather sections up in elastic bands for a tie-dye effect **(2)**.

**Dye.** Wearing plastic gloves, place the fabric into the turmeric dye bath making sure it is completely submerged. The longer you leave it the more vibrant the colour will be. When you are happy with the colour, remove, unfold and rinse til the water runs clear. Once the fabric is dry, it is ready to use.

*"Beetroot, or avocado skins and seeds, give a beautiful array of pinkish hues. Red cabbage is good for blues and for orange try onion skins and carrots."*

# Bunny Wrap

This project is an adorable heirloom piece to use again and again. Perfect for Easter and spring birthdays.

**Make the gift box.** Copy the template (*see Templates*) onto card and make up the box as instructed.

**Cut the fabric pieces.** I've used a Liberty Tana Lawn for the headscarf and a thin grey viscose fabric for the bunny. From the grey fabric cut one large triangle measuring 35 x 70cm (13¾ x 27½in) for the face and one small triangle measuring 24 x 44cm (9½ x 17¼in) for the head; and from the patterned fabric cut a 20 x 74cm (8 x 29in) rectangle for the scarf **(1)**.

**Mark the centre points.** Fold the headscarf rectangle in half to find the centre. Mark with pins, left and right. Repeat with the triangles and pin the long edges, lining all the pins up **(2)**.

**Join the fabrics.** Place the triangle for the face right-side down on top of the scarf rectangle making sure the two marker pins line up. Pin in place **(3)**. Join with a 5mm (¼in) seam allowance, sewing with a straight stitch and then a zig zag one to prevent fraying. Repeat with the triangle for the head. Open the fabric out and press. On a flat surface trim the joined fabrics into a square **(4)**. You should only need to trim the scarf rectangle.

## You will need

- Two thin fabrics: one in a bunny colour and a patterned one for the headscarf
- Pink fabric for ears, 12 x 12cm (4¾ x 4¾in)
- Fusible webbing, 12 x 12 cm (4¾ x 4¾in)
- Two buttons for eyes, embroidery threads and an air-erasable pen to make the face
- Card

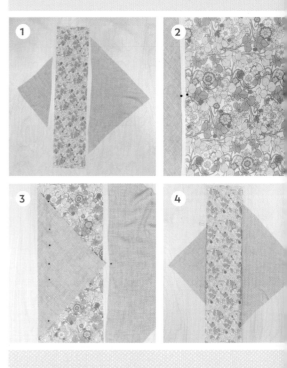

*"For a finishing touch add a hand embroidered name to the bunny's headscarf "*

**Hem the wrap.** Trim the two grey corners into a gentle curve for ears. Turn and press a 1cm (⅜in) hem around the scarf and face parts, by pinning and then sewing with a small zig zag stitch. Flip the wrap over and repeat the hem for the head triangle. This means there will be no wrong sides showing when the wrap is knotted.

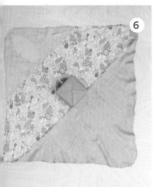

**Make the inner ears.** Iron the pink rectangle to the fusible webbing (*see Techniques: Fusible Web*). Use the template to cut two bunny ears (*see Templates*). With the fabric square right-side up place the first inner ear on the face triangle 1.5cm (⅝in) down from the top of the ear, iron in place. Turn the fabric over and similarly position the second ear on the head triangle. Iron in place. Zig zag stitch the ears in place **(5)**.

**Wrap the giftbox.** With the fabric on a flat surface right-side down place the gift box on the fabric so the front edge of the box sits centrally on the seam line between the scarf and the face triangle **(6)**.

**Tie the wrap.** Take the grey corners and tie a single knot on top of the box **(7)**. Next take the headscarf corners and bring up to the top front of the box and tie a reef knot (*see Reef Knot*). Manipulate the fabric so the ears are both facing forward and the headscarf looks neat **(8)**. Finally add the face: mark the position of the eyes and nose with an air-erasable pen. Undo the wrap, sew on the eye buttons and embroider a nose and whiskers in pink thread. You can add a little pink rouge or paint for rosy cheeks.

*"These measurements and templates work for my gift box. If you want to make different sized bunnies then adjust the measurements accordingly."*

# Bottle Sleeves

These bottle holders are inspired by my friend and crocheter extraordinaire Katie Jones. She creates whole Aran jumpers in this style and they are things of beauty.

## You will need

- Thick knit jumpers, Aran ones are perfect
- Chunky yarn in different colours
- Yarn needle
- Fork

**Remove the arms.** Turn your jumper inside out and then insert your gift into one sleeve. Cut the sleeve approx 5cm (2in) further down than the bottom of the gift. You need to make sure the sleeve will gather comfortably around the base of the gift.

**Sew a drawstring.** Using a piece of yarn sew a running stitch around the raw edge of the sleeve then pull the two ends to gather. Tie a tight double knot to (6 x 4in) secure the drawstring and trim the excess yarn. Turn the sleeve right-side out.

**Decorate.** The design you sew will depend on the style of your jumper, my favourite stitches to use are: back stitch, French knots and miniature pompoms (*see Techniques: Embroidery Stitches and Fork Pompoms*).

**Make a small bobble hat.** To completely disguise your gift, cut a 15 x 10cm (6 x 4in) piece of jumper that includes both ribbing and the body of the jumper. Sew the raw edges together and work a running stitch along the top. Gather the running stitch and secure with a knot. Add a pompom and decorative stitching, then turn the ribbing up to create the brim of the hat.

*"The rest of the jumper can be used to make more bottle holders or a jumper pouch (see next project)."*

# Jumper Pouch

Look for jumpers with an obvious purl stitch and then create your own patterns using a simple duplicate stitch.

## You will need

- Thick jumper with obvious purl stitch (which makes little 'v's on one side and little zig zags on the other)
- Two buttons
- A selection of DK yarns and a yarn needle

**Cut the jumper.** Turn the jumper inside out and place it on a flat surface so the body side seams line up. Measure and cut your pouch to size (*remember the ribbed waist of the jumper will become the top of the pouch*). Pin the sides and base of the pouch together.

**Make the pouch.** With a 1cm (⅜in) seam allowance sew around the jumper. Start and stop at the point where the ribbed waist begins. Trim then sew with a zig zag stitch to stop the knit fraying **(1)**.

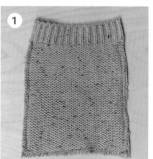
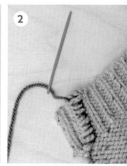

**Sew the waistband.** Secure the fraying edges of the waistband by turning over 5mm (¼in) and sewing with an overstitch **(2)**. When starting, sew a couple of stitches to secure the yarn but leave a 3cm (1¼in) tail. Then overstitch this tail, hiding it within the turned fabric. To make it invisible, use yarn unravelled from another part of the jumper.

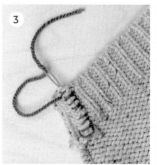

**Finish the pouch.** Feed the needle down through the row of stitches to secure the loose end of wool then cut **(3)**. Turn the jumper right side out. If you are using the full width of the jumper, just unpick the side seams to the depth of the waistband and finish as above.

*"This cuddly gift pouch could have a second life as a cushion cover or pyjama case."*

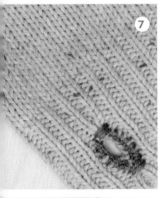

**Add the buttons.** Fold the front waistband down so it goes into the pouch **(4)**. Position the two buttons on the front of the jumper, fold the back flap down over the buttons making sure it covers them. Sew the buttons in place.

**Create the button holes.** Begin the button hole with a couple of long stitches of yarn, joining two of the ribbed sections together **(5)**.

**Blanket stitch.** Sew a close row of blanket stitch the length of the button hole (*see Techniques: Embroidery Stitches*), sewing two stitches in each hole of knitting **(6)**. Repeat the long stitches and blanket stitch down the other side of the button hole. Finish by inserting the needle into the stitches on the reverse side. Carefully cut the wool strands within the buttonhole to open it up **(7)**. If buttonholes seem too fiddly use a couple of poppers instead. Sew one half of the poppers in place of the button and the other on the underside of the flap. Sew a button on the front of the flap for decoration.

**Add the duplicate stitch decoration.** Embellish the jumper pouch, as shown opposite, by adding a stitched decoration in your chosen colour of yarn (*see Techniques: Duplicate Stitch*).

*"Try embroidering the recipient's initials onto the pouch for a truly personal touch."*

# Pocket Pockets

This is a speedy creation that uses breast pockets from jackets and shirts. The best ones come with a buttoned flap.

## You will need

- Clothing with patch breast pockets
- Fusible web
- Pinking shears
- Air-erasable pen (optional)
- Embroidery needle and threads

**Pockets made from thicker fabrics, such as denim or corduroy.** Use fusible web to hem thick fabric as the layers won't fit under your sewing machine foot. Trim round the pocket to give a 2cm (¾in) seam allowance. Cut strips of fusible web (*see Techniques: Fusible Web*) and iron on to the reverse of the seam allowance. Using pinking shears cut the edges of the fabric. Trim the corners at a diagonal to reduce bulk. Fold each side onto the reverse and iron in place **(1)**.

**Pockets made from thinner fabrics, such as chambray or cotton.** Prepare the pocket as above with a 2cm (¾in) seam allowance all round. Turn and press a double hem, fold onto the reverse of the pocket, pin and either hand or machine sew in place **(2)**.

**Embroider to decorate.** Go freestyle or sketch out an embroidery design with an air-erasable pen (*see Techniques: Embroidery Stitches*).

**Visible mending.** If the pocket has any holes, just trim away any frayed strands then mend it with a piece of contrasting fabric about 2cm (¾in) larger than the hole on all sides, see Techniques: Visible Mending.

*"If your pockets seems little flimsy cut pieces of card to fit and insert inside."*

# Pyjama Party Bags

Old pyjama bottoms make great gift bags. The addition of a gusset at the base makes them look more sophisticated than just a pair of cut-up pjs!

## You will need

- Pyjamas or soft trousers
- Thin cardboard

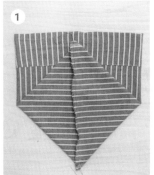

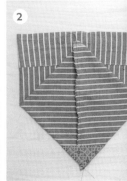

**Start at the bottom.** Measure the height of the bag from the cuffs upwards plus 5cm (2in). The cuffs will become the top of the bags. For a matching pair of bags cut both trouser legs.

**Pin and sew the bottom.** Turn inside out, pin and sew with a 1cm (⅜in) seam allowance. If you want to make stronger French seams, follow the instructions in the Shirt Pouches project.

**Create the gusset at the base.** Manipulate the bag so the side seams now lie in the middle of the bag and the corners create a square shape **(1)**. To make sure both sides of the base are equal you can use a cardboard triangle as a template. Place as shown **(2)** and draw a line along the straight edge. Pin then sew. Repeat with the second corner.

**Turn the bag right-side out.** Press the base of the bag so the creases are defined. If your pyjamas had a drawstring remove it from the waistband and use as the tie to secure the bag. Otherwise use a piece of ribbon or fabric twine (*see Fabric Twine*).

*"Pyjama bottoms are perfect for making gift bags. Any spare fabric could be used to make fabric twine, pompoms or tassels to decorate."*

# Shirt Pouches

The button plackets on shirts offer a
perfect closure for these gift pouches.

**Prepare the fabric.** With the shirt on a flat surface and
buttons done up measure and cut rectangles through
both layers of fabric. Ideally you will have at least
three buttons on each pouch. Make sure you have at
least 2cm (¾in) of fabric either side of the first and
last button **(1)**.

**Create French seams.** Undo the middle button of your
pouch then pin the shirt back and front together right-
side out **(2)**.

**Sew and trim.** Sew around all four edges of the
rectangle with a 5mm (¼in) seam allowance. Carefully
trim this down to 3mm (⅛in) **(3)**.

**Turn right-side in.** Use the shirt opening to turn the
pouch right sides in. Press then sew a second seam
around the bag with a 1cm (⅜in) seam allowance to
encase the raw edges inside the seam **(4)**. Turn the
pouch right side out again and press. Decorate with
any bright badges or iron-on patches you have in your
haberdashery stash.

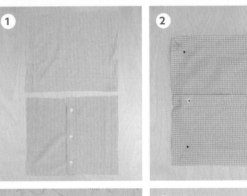

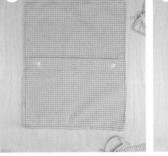

*"This project is great
for practicing your
French seams."*

# Shirt Cuff Purses

These little purses are so clever. Just the right size for gift cards and small trinkets.

## You will need

- Shirt with buttoned cuffs
- Stitch unpicker

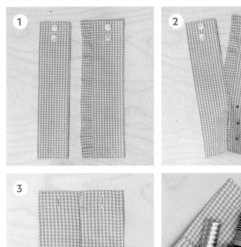

**To make a double cuff purse.** Remove both cuffs from the shirt. Remove one by unpicking the seam that joins it to the sleeve. Cut the second one leaving 2cm (¾in) of sleeve fabric intact **(1)**.

**Join the two cuffs.** Undo both cuffs and lay them flat. Taking the first cuff with the sleeve fabric attached, insert the fabric into the open seam of the second cuff **(2)**. Try to get the edges of the cuffs as close together as possible. Pin along the join then sew.

**Make the purse.** Fold the cuffs up to create a purse. With the button side uppermost. Pin together then sew each side from the base of the purse to the opening **(3)**.

**To make a single cuff purse.** Make smaller purses by using a single cuff. Detach it from the sleeve with a stitch unpicker, then fold and pin into a purse shape. Machine sew up each side. You will need to sew the full length of the side removed from the sleeve to secure.

*"Replace the buttons with pretty mismatched ones from your stash"*

# Shirt Gift Bags

This drawstring bag can be made in every size from giant Santa sacks right down to small jewellery gift bags.

## You will need
**to make a 20 x 22cm (8 x 8½in) size bag**

- 2 fabric rectangles, 30 x 24cm (12 x 9½in)
- 2 fabric strips, 4 x 80cm (1½ x 31½in)
- Large yarn needle

**Create the bag.** Place the fabrics wrong sides together and pin. Mark 10cm (4in) down from the top of the bag on both sides **(1)**. Continue to make French seams (*see instructions in Shirt Pouches project*) from the 10cm (4in) mark.

**Create the drawstring channel.** Turn and press a 1cm (⅜in) seam allowance at the bag top of both pieces of fabric **(2)**. Turn the top of the bag down till it meets the beginning of the side seams. Press then pin. On both sides of the bag sew a seam 5mm (¼in) up from the top hem that you created in step one. Sew a second seam 15mm (⅝in) up from that **(3)**.

**Make the drawstrings.** Take the two long strips of fabric, turn a 15mm (⅝in) seam allowance at each of the short edges. Fold each strip in half lengthways and press. Open out, then carefully fold each of the sides in towards the pressed line. Press then fold in half again, press again. Machine sew along the open edge of the fabric **(4)**.

**Complete the bag.** Thread one drawstring onto the yarn needle. Thread through the drawstring channel so it starts and finishes on the same side. Repeat with the second string from the other side. Knot ends together.

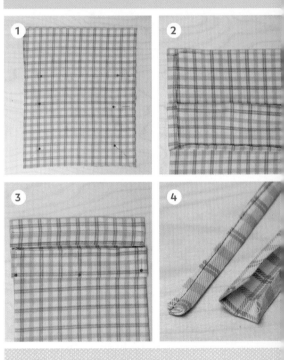

*"Use items of clothing from different family members to create bags with real meaning."*

# Odd Sock Crackers

Where do socks go? If you, like me, have a bag of sad odd socks this project is ideal for using them up.

## You will need

- A selection of odd socks (2 per cracker)
- Needle and thin crochet thread or similar
- Small plastic bottle or cardboard tube
- Debobbler (if your socks have gone a bit fuzzy from too many washes!)

**Take two socks.** Starting at the top cut both socks to the same length. If that's not possible that's okay, your cracker join will just be off centre). With my ankle socks I can get about a 14cm (5½in) length before the sock starts to change shape for the ankle. Keeping one sock tube right side out turn the second one inside out and slip over the first, lining up the raw edges **(1)**.

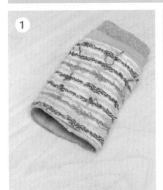

**Pin the raw edges together, keeping the tube shape.** Then sew with a 1cm (⅜in) seam allowance. Trim away the excess material and turn right sides out.

**Make the drawstrings.** Measure about 7cm (2⅜in) from the top of both ends of the tube. Using a long running stitch sew around the tube with the needle and embroidery thread. Leave around 15cm (6in) of thread at either end **(2)**.

**Pull the threads tight.** Tighten the threads at one end of the sock to gather the fabric, then tie a bow. Cut a 10cm (4in) tube from a plastic bottle and insert it into the sock. Fill with gifts and then close by pulling the threads tight and tying a second bow.

*"These crackers were made with a pair of medium sized socks and a small plastic bottle. Children's socks would work well using a toilet roll."*

# Jumper Cuff Bags

These mini gift bags are made from the sleeves and waistband of a thin knit jumper – the ribbed edge makes a decorative cuff.

## You will need

- Thin knit jumper with cuffs
- Needle and thread

**Start with the cuffs.** With the jumper inside out, laid flat and the cuff folded, decide on the length of your gift bag and cut the sleeve away from the jumper in a straight line. Before you cut remember to add a 1cm (⅜in) seam allowance to your measurement.

**Rearrange the seam line.** Manipulate the cut fabric so the seam of the jumper lies down the back of the bag. Pin the raw edges together and sew **(1)**. Turn right side out and lightly press if necessary. Repeat with the second sleeve.

**Next use the waistband.** Decide on the finished width and height of your gift bag. Double the width and add 1cm (⅜in) for the seam allowance to the height and width. Cut a rectangle from the jumper using the ribbed edge of the jumper as the top.

**Fold the fabric in half right sides together.** Pin down the side seam then sew. Manipulate the fabric as before so the sewn seam lies centrally down the back of the bag, pin the bottom raw edges together and sew. Turn right side out and press lightly. Add a bow (*see Odd Sock Bows*) to close **(2)**.

*"The bags I've made here are all about 10cm (4in) high and are great for small gifts like hair accessories, jewellery or bars of soap."*

# THE EXTRAS

If brown paper packages are your favourite thing, make a few of these finishing touches to add pizzazz and reduce your scrap bag

# Odd Sock Bows

These bows are easy to make with a little cutting and hand stitching. They also double up as an extra present for anyone with long hair.

## You will need

- Odd or old socks
- Hair elastics

**Turn the sock inside out.** From the foot part cut an 8cm (3in) wide tube. Pull the raw edges together so the tube ends up about 4cm (8⅝in) wide. Hand stitch the two raw edges together **(1)**. Turn right-side out, hiding the seam, then flatten into a rectangle.

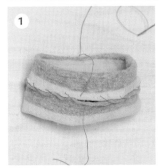

**Make the bow shape.** Wrap a length of thread around the centre of the rectangle several times, pulling tightly to create a bow shape **(2)**.

**Add the hair elastic.** Having created the bow shape place one hair elastic on top of the thread. Continue wrapping the thread around the bow and the hair elastic to secure the elastic in place. Fasten with a knot.

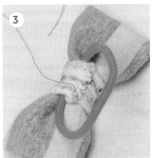

**Make the middle.** Cut a 2 x 5cm (¾ x 2in) piece of sock, roll the raw edges inwards. With the raw edges hidden wrap around the centre of the bow and the hair elastic hiding the thread. Carefully turn the end to hide the raw edges so the fabric is tight and hand stitch in place **(3)**.

*"These bows could also be added to hair clips or brooch backs and still used as present fastenings."*

# T-shirt Tassels

T-shirt yarn is available commercially in big rolls but it's super easy to make your own for free with your old t-shirts.

## You will need

- T-shirts (all-over patterns work well)
- Per tassel: one 30 x 15cm (12 x 6in) rectangle, two 2 x 40cm (¾ x 15¾in) strips, or the longest length you can get from your t-shirt

**Fold t-shirt rectangle in half.** Cut 2cm (¾in) wide strips stopping 2cm (¾in) from the fold. Pull each strip to make the fabric curl into tubes **(1)**. See Techniques: Tights Elastic for the same method applied to old tights - it works brilliantly for t-shirt fabric too!

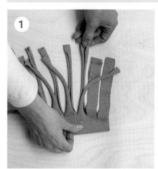
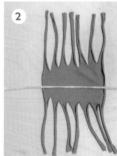

**Open the rectangle flat.** Place one of the longer strips of t-shirt in the middle **(2)**.

**Gather and secure.** Tie a knot with the long strip, gathering the tassel as you tighten it. Tie a second knot to secure. Take the second strip and place it around the tassel 3cm (1¼in) from the top. Create a loop shape with the short end **(3)**.

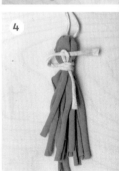

**Wrap the tassel.** Wind the strip around the tassel over the loop a few times. On the final wrap thread the end through the loop **(4)**, then pull the loop tail which will pull the loop under the wrap securing the two tails. Trim.

*"Make multi-coloured tassels by layering up two different coloured rectangles and cutting strips from each."*

# Fabric Pompoms

I love this alternative to the traditional wool pompom. I find them incredibly addictive to make.

## You will need

- Thin cardboard
- Cut or torn strips of fabric about 2cm (¾in) wide and as long as your items of clothing will allow. Thin summer weight shirts, dresses, and trousers work well.

**Make the pompom makers.** From thin cardboard cut two donut shapes approximately 7cm (2¾in) diameter. Cut the inner hole about 3cm (1¼in) diameter. Cut a slit in both **(1)**.

**Place the two donuts together.** Wrap with the fabric strips. For the multi-coloured effect wrap three or four strips at the same time **(2)**. Stop when the makers are full and you can't see through the middle hole.

**Open the pompom.** Cut around the edge of the pompom with scissors to reveal the cardboard discs **(3)**.

**Finish the pompom.** Carefully separate the pompom discs slightly and wrap two lengths of fabric around the centre of the pompom **(4)**. Tie to secure with a tight double knot. Remove the makers and trim into a spherical shape. Twist the fabric ties together into twine (*see Fabric Twine*).

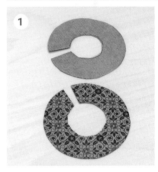

*"These joyous fabric pompoms are perfect present toppers. They also look great strung together as garlands or tree ornaments."*

# Fabric Twine

I was so excited when I worked out how to make this twine. It's a very mindful occupation as the twisting of the fabric becomes quite meditative.

**Prepare the twine.** Knot two 50cm (20in) long strips of fabric together then shut the knot into a heavy drawer or secure it to a solid object. Tie a pencil centrally to the other end of each strip.

**Twist the first strip.** Starting with one strip twist and twist and twist till the strip is almost coiling up on itself. I find twisting the pencil with one hand and gently guiding the fabric with the other works well **(1)**.

**Twist the second strip.** This can be a little tricky. Repeat the twisting action with the second strip whilst keeping the first strip twisted. A heavy weight on the first pencil will stop it coming untwisted.

**Twist together.** Release your hold on the strips and they will intertwine with each other. They may need a little coaxing and manipulating to create an even twist.

**Make it longer.** Add more strips of fabric by tying the new to the old with a reef knot (*see Reef Knot*) **(2)**.

*"Teamwork makes the dream work! Two people could work on this twine at the same time, each person in charge of one pencil."*

# Scrap Bunting

This elasticated bunting removes the need for sellotape if you have some gifts that need to be wrapped in paper.

## You will need

- Thin elastic or tights elastic (see Techniques: Tights Elastic)
- Scrap fabric rectangles
- Fusible web
- Rotary cutter and ruler, or scissors
- Yarn needle (optional)

**Make the flags.** Cut 15 fabric scraps into 4 x 8cm (1½ x 3¼in) rectangles. Place the rectangles right side up onto a sheet of fusible web and iron to fix (*see Techniques: Fusible Web*) **(1)**.

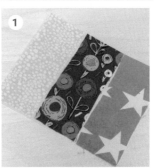
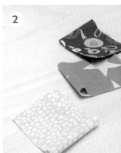

**Fold in half.** Remove the fusible web protective paper then separate the rectangles and fold each neatly in half.

**Iron together.** Carefully iron each of the flags to activate the glue. Make sure you don't iron the last 5mm (¼in) at the fold of the flag to create a channel for the elastic to pass through **(2)**.

**Cut the V shape.** Using a rotary cutter and ruler (*or steady hands and scissors*) cut a V shape at the base of each flag **(3)**.

**Assemble the bunting.** Thread the flags onto the elastic. If using elastic made from tights you may find this easier if you thread the elastic onto a yarn needle **(4)**.

*"Use decorative pinking shears and circles of fabric to make pretty scallop shaped bunting."*

# Alphabet Gift Tags

The basis for these letter-shaped gift tags are the thick cord handles from old paper gift bags. Once made you can manipulate the cords into all sorts of shapes.

**Reinforce the cord.** Starting at one end, twist the fuse wire around the cord. The wire goes around the cord rather than the other way round to give a smoother result. When you reach the end of the cord twist the wire and go back the other way **(1)**.

**Wrap in fabric.** Place the cord on the fabric about 2cm (¾in) down from one short edge. Fold this edge over covering the end of the cord and fix in place with a little glue **(2)**. Begin twisting the fabric around the cord, catch the raw edges of the end as you twist and secure with a little glue if necessary **(3)**. Continue winding the fabric around the cord, keeping the tension tight so the fabric doesn't go all baggy. Finish off the end with glue making sure you secure all raw edges so it looks neat.

**Shape the letter.** Decide on what letter you wish to make (*follow the alphabet at the end of this book for guidance*). Bend the cord to create the letter shape. Don't worry if you need to try a couple of times to get the shape right – practice makes perfect **(4)**.

## You will need

- Cord, approx 40cm (15¾in) per letter
- Thin fuse wire
- Strips of fabric 2 x 50cm (¾ x 20in)
- Fabric glue or glue gun

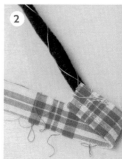
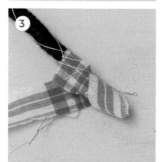

*"If your paper bags still have some life in them but you want to make these letters, then replace the cords on the bags with strips of pretty fabric."*

# Flower Toppers

A bright bunch of fabric flowers looks wonderful atop a gift. Thread them onto elastic and the topper can double up as a flower crown for the recipient.

## You will need

- Various thin fabrics, old chiffon scarves, camisoles or summer dresses
- Needle and thread
- Waterproof inks and paint brushes (optional)

**Cut rectangles.** Cut them in different sizes from all the fabrics. A good size to start with is 6 x 30cm (2⅜ x 12in). The longer the rectangle the more petals you can make.

**Make concertinas.** Fold each rectangle into an even concertina. If the fabric is slippery press lightly with an iron to keep the folds. Vary the width of the folds across the different rectangles **(1)**.

**Cut petal shapes.** Keeping the fabric folded, cut curved or pointed shapes. Stop cutting about 1cm (½in) from the bottom of the fabric **(2)**.

**Sew a line of running stitch.** Make running stitches about 5mm (¼in) up from the bottom edge. Pull the ends of the thread to gather the fabric. Manipulate the petals to create a flower shape **(3)**.

**Create mega blooms.** Join two different flower types together by inserting one inside the other. You may need to loosen the knot of the outer flower slightly to get the inner one to sit inside. Sew a couple of stitches through all layers of fabric to secure **(4)**.

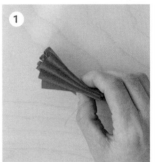

*"No patterned fabric? No worries. Make large brush strokes and splatters of ink across the fabric before you make the flowers."*

# Fabric Gift Tags

These gift tags are created using pieces of crumb quilting – a great way to use up scraps. I've explained the method in the Crumb Quilt Wrap Project.

### You will need

- Fusible web
- Eyelet kit
- Crumb quilted patchwork fabric, 14 x 11cm (5½ x 4¼in)
- Pale coloured fabric, 6 x 7cm (2⅜ x 2¾in)

**To make one tag.** Fix fusible web to the back of the piece of crumb quilt fabric (*see Crumb Quilt Wrap*) **(1)**.

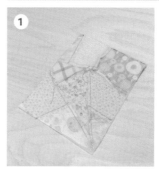
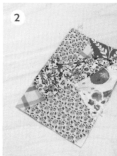

**Remove the protective paper.** Fold in half widthways and iron to glue together **(2)**.

**Make a point.** Draw a 2cm (¾in) deep triangle at one short edge. Use pinking shears to trim all edges **(3)**.

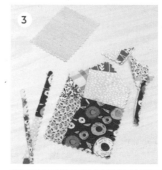

**Add the address panel.** Fix fusible web to the reverse of the pale fabric then trim all edges with pinking shears. Place onto the crumb quilt fabric and iron in place. Machine sew a row of topstitch around the rectangle.

**Add an eyelet.** Insert an eyelet in the top of the triangle **(4)**. Alternatively you could cut a hole with scissors or make a small button hole (*for buttonhole instructions see Jumper Pouch project*). Add a length of fabric twine (*see Fabric Twine*) or ribbon to each tag.

"*Small rubber stamps and ink are perfect for addressing these gift tags. Beware fibre-tipped pens as they bleed.*"

# Ribbon Rosettes

These rosettes are a great way of using old ribbons from previous gifts or fancy purchases.

## You will need

- 1m (1yd) of 3cm (1¼in) wide ribbon. This can be made up of separate pieces
- Needle and thread
- Glue gun (optional)
- Safety pin or hair elastic

**Prepare the ribbon.** Iron the ribbon flat. Cut two 18cm (7in), two 16cm (6¼in), and one 10cm (4in) length.

**Make the loops.** Fold one piece of ribbon in half lengthways and pinch to mark the centre. Take one end and twist it to the centre point to create a pointed loop. Secure in place with glue or a couple of stitches **(1)**. Repeat with the other end—twisting the opposite way so the ribbon makes a figure of eight shape—and also with both ends of the other three ribbon pieces.

**Create the centre.** Sew a small running stitch along one long edge of the 10cm (4in) ribbon **(2)**. Pull the thread to gather the ribbon into a flower shape. Knot to secure.

**Build the rosette.** Place the two larger ribbons on top of each other so the loops form a star **(3)**. Fix in place. Repeat with the two smaller loops, nestling them inside the larger ones so the points are staggered. Fix in place.

**Finish.** Fix the flower in the centre and add a tail using the remainder of the ribbon, trimmed into a V shape **(4)**. Fix a safety pin or hair elastic to the back to attach the rosette to gifts.

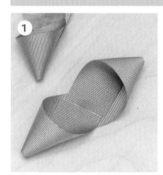

*"You can use any width of ribbon for this project. Experiment with strips of paper till you get the optimum loop length."*

# Techniques

## EMBROIDERY STITCHES

### 1. Back Stitch

Bring up your needle from underneath your fabric at **(A)**, stitch backwards to **(B)** and then bring your needle out at **(C)**. Insert the needle back at **(A)**, and continue along the line.

### 2. Twisted Running Stitch

Sew a row of running stitch, then, with a contrasting coloured thread, bring up your needle from the back of the fabric and weave through the stitches. Do not sew through any fabric as you go.

### 3. Split Stitch

Working with a stranded embroidery floss, bring up your needle from underneath your fabric and make a back stitch, insert the needle at **(D)** through the middle of the previous stitch, splitting the thread. Bring the needle back up at **(E)** and continue along the line.

### 4. Blanket Stitch

Bring up your needle from the back of the fabric at **(F)**. Insert the needle at **(G)** and bring it out at **(H)** Make sure you loop the thread around your needle before you complete the stitch.

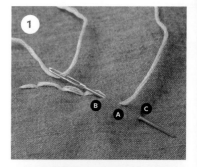

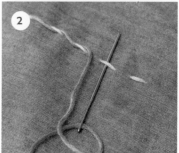

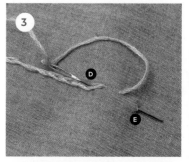

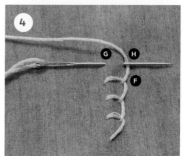

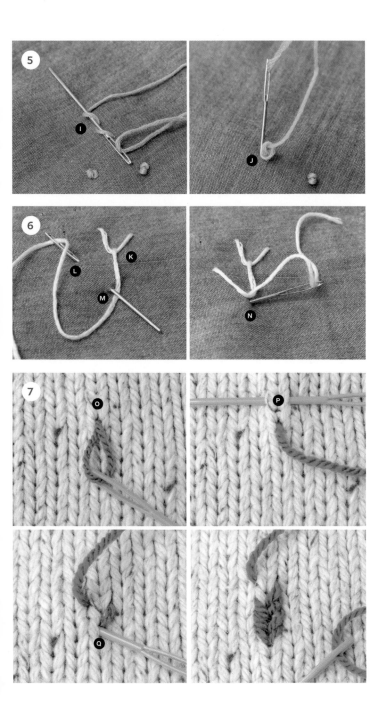

## 5. French Knot

Bring your needle up from the back of your fabric then hold it flat on the fabric and wrap the thread around the needle twice (not too tightly) **(I)**. Gently pull the needle through the thread loops and slide them down the thread on to the fabric. Insert the needle back into the fabric close to the original stitch **(J)**.

## 6. Open Scallop

Bring your needle up from the back of the fabric at **(K)** and then stitch back into the fabric **(L)**, bringing the needle out at **(M)** at the same time. Pull the needle through the fabric and wrap the thread around the needle and pull to create a loop. Return the needle into the fabric at **(N)**.

## 7. Duplicate Stitch

*Use this technique to embellish knits with motifs or even mend small holes.*

Come up through the knitting at the bottom of the V stitch you wish to duplicate **(O)**.

Slide the needle behind the V stitch that is directly above the one you are covering **(P)**.

Insert the needle back into the knitting at **(Q)**.

Repeat, keeping the tension tight, but not so tight that it gathers the existing knitting up.

# VISIBLE MENDING

*This is my favourite way of fixing rips and holes in clothing. The extra layer of fabric reinforces the rip for the future.*

**1.** Tidy up the rip or hole you are fixing by trimming away any frayed bits and loose strands.

**2.** On the reverse, pin then tack a second piece of fabric. Make sure this fabric is at least 2cm (¾in) larger than the rip. For extra stability fix with fusible web around the edges of the hole.

**3.** Join the two fabrics with seed stitches. Seed stitch is a small individual running stitch worked in random patterns and directions.

**4.** Use a selection of different coloured threads. When finished remove the tacking thread and press.

# FUSIBLE WEB

*Known in some parts of the world as Bondaweb and in others as Wonder Under, this product allows you to iron on fabric shapes easily.*

**5.** Cut a rough shape from the fusible web and place rough side down on the wrong side of the fabric.

**6.** Iron for 5 seconds. Cut the fabric out precisely then remove paper backing.

**7.** Place coated side down on second piece of fabric, cover with a damp cloth, press for 10 seconds

**8.** Finish with a decorative zig zag stitch if applicable.

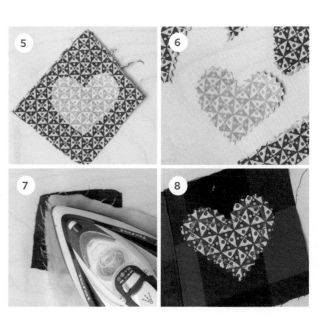

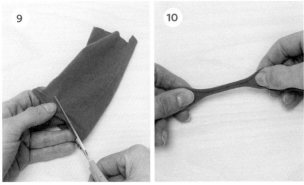

## TIGHTS ELASTIC

*Old tights are perfect for securing gifts instead of tape. Cut 3cm (1¼in) widths to create loops, or follow these instructions for longer lengths.*

**9.** With your scissors at an angle cut continuously around the tights leg.

**10.** Using both hands pull the lengths of tights apart so they roll up and the raw edges are hidden.

*"If you have a t-shirt with no side seams you can make loads of t-shirt yarn using this technique."*

## FORK POMPOMS

*Make irresistible little pompoms with this simple method – all you need is a humble fork.*

**11.** Cut 15cm (6in) of yarn, and place it between the middle two tines of a fork.

**12.** Wind the yarn 50 times around the fork keeping the beginning of yarn free.

**13.** Use the beginning yarn to gather the wound yarn tightly and tie a double knot. Slide off the fork.

**14.** Cut each side of the bundle so the wool is released then trim the pompom to tidy it.

# Templates

All templates are shown here at 50%. You can download full-size versions of these templates from **www.davidandcharles.com**.

## Bunny wrap

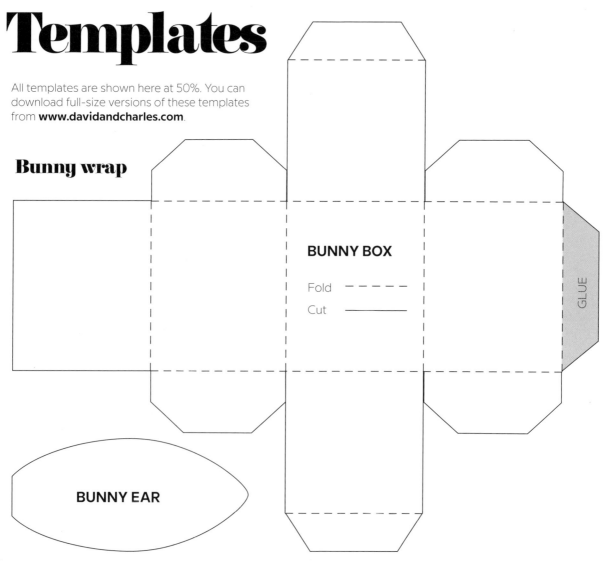

**BUNNY BOX**

Fold - - - - -

Cut ————

**BUNNY EAR**

## Alphabet Gift Tags

A B C D E F G H I J K L M
N O P Q R S T U V W X Y Z

# SUPPLIERS

Run out of things to cut up in your own wardrobe? Then these are the next best thing:

**Friends and neighbours.** Asking for donations is a great way to gather interesting fabric for projects. It will save your friends and neighbours a trip to the charity shop, and if you promise to return their cast-offs transformed into a gift wrap with a bottle of wine inside, I'm sure you'll see the donations flooding in!

**Charity Shops.** High Street charity shops are a great place to shop, look for extra large garments for maximum fabric gain.

**Kilo Sales.** Kilo sales are a relatively new way of buying vintage and second hand clothes. As the name suggests you pay by the kilo, so while big jumpers and denim can cost more, you can get an awful lot of thin scarves for not many pennies. Both Pre Loved Kilo (www.Prelovedkilo.com) and The Kilo Sale (www.thekilosale.com) have regular events round the UK.

If you really want a special piece of fabric or pretty notion to finish off your gifts then these small independent suppliers are wonderful:

**Cloudcraft.co.uk** Lots of lovely ribbons and threads and the place to go for 100% wool felt.

**Clothandcandy.co.uk** Beautiful printed cottons from all over the world.

**Cottonclara.com** A beautiful mix of handmade embroidery and cross stitch kits and haberdashery supplies.

**Newcrafthouse.com** All the beautiful fabrics here are designer deadstock – destined for landfill or stored away for years and forgotten about. It's a constantly changing line up of fabrics.

**Textilegarden.com** All the buttons you could ever want including a lovely selection of eco and recycled ones.

# INSPIRATION

My favourite social media is Instagram, I find it inspiring and love connecting with people on a visual level. Here are some great accounts to follow all doing their thing for the environment:

**@sewyeah** Me! And my craft-filled life.

**@steelandstitch** Emma produces awesome clothing and crochet hacks. If you want to turn your duvet cover into a pair of dungarees then Emma's your girl.

**@katiejonesknits** Crazy and colourful knitting and crochet patterns. Katie is a strong supporter of workers' rights in the fashion industry and is all about sustainability.

**@enbrogue** A brilliant account full of tips on how to live a more sustainable life, from clothes shopping to vegetable patches.

**@makeitbettermag** Conscientious crafting for the modern maker. Full of inspiring makes and how-tos all with a 'reduce, reuse, recycle' vibe.

**@makesmthng** Greenpeace's crafty cousin - using maker-power to fight overconsumption.

**@itsrooper** If you've been bitten by the Furoshiki bug then go one step further and purchase one of these beautiful bags from Natasha. All the bags are made from remnants and vintage fabrics.

**@adele.d.riley** Incredible works of art using upcycled fabrics.

# All the thank yous there ever were to...

everyone at David and Charles for helping get this book out the door so quickly! To Sarah for contacting me via Instagram with the intriguing proposition in the first place. To Anna, Jess and Jane for making sure the book looked great and that words were spelled correctly. To Jason whose two-hour video call photography tutorial enabled me to take my camera off auto for the first time ever and whose post-production wizardry made my photos sparkle. To Emma, Hannah and Keiko for helping me with eco stats and Japanese terminology.

My family – Mum and Dad, Jo, Ian, Oli and Elliot – this will be the year our Christmas is totally paper-free! To Jake, Matt, Lottie, Hannah, Kirsty and Laura for the encouragement and support, and all my neighbours for their clothes donations when supplies ran low.

And finally to all of you who are doing something, anything, to make this world a more sustainable place to live – you are all brilliant!

## ABOUT THE AUTHOR

Christine Leech is an author, designer, maker, stylist, and workshop host. She won her first craft-related award at just 5 years old (best hemmed handkerchief in the village Flower Show). This led to a life filled with cardboard, fabric, scissors and glue.

Zero Waste Gift Wrap is her tenth book – having written others on many different craft subjects including pompoms, papercraft, embroidery and sewing for the home.

She lives by the adage 'A Creative Mess is Better Than Idle Tidiness' which gives her the excuse to never tidy up! She documents her crafty life on her Instagram @sewyeah, where she shares daily inspiration, step-by-step projects and videos.

# Index

A DAVID AND CHARLES BOOK
© David and Charles, Ltd 2020

David and Charles is an imprint of David and Charles, Ltd
1 Emperor Way, Exeter Business Park, Exeter, EX1 3QS

Text and Designs © Christine Leech 2020
Layout and Photography © David and Charles, Ltd 2020

First published in the UK and USA in 2020

A catalogue record for this book is available from the
British Library.

ISBN-13: 9781446308431 paperback

ISBN-13: 9781446308431 EPUB

We have considered the environmental
impact of this book by using soy-based inks,
printing on FSC paper and using unbleached,
uncoated duplex board for the front cover.

Printed in China by Asia Pacific for:
David and Charles, Ltd
1 Emperor Way, Exeter Business Park,
Exeter, EX1 3QS

10 9 8 7 6 5 4 3 2 1

Senior Commissioning Editor: Sarah Callard

Managing Editor: Jessica Cropper

Project Editor: Jane Trollope

Design Manager: Anna Wade

Pre-press Designer: Ali Stark

Book Layout and Design:
Anna Wade and Christine Leech

Art Direction and Photography:
Christine Leech

Production Manager: Beverley Richardson

David and Charles publishes high-quality
books on a wide range of subjects.
For more information visit
www.davidandcharles.com.

Layout of the digital edition of this book
may vary depending on reader hardware
and display settings.